Selling Eyewear in the 21st Century

Introduction

As an employer, it is your responsibility to make sure that your staff is properly trained and unless you have extensive sales experience, it can be a daunting task.

As a business owner, you invest thousands of dollars in the best equipment, décor, quality materials and advertising. You offer your customers the latest in fashion eyewear as well as designer frames, premium lenses and lens treatments, yet the most important part of your business is the one most often overlooked, your staff.

Why are you in business? What is the goal of your business?

Is it your goal to provide quality eyecare?
Is it your goal to provide exceptional customer service?
Is it your goal to service your customers?
The answer is a resounding NO!!!

Those things are merely the route you need to take to get to the real goal of any business. Throughout this course, I refer to the consumer as a customer, not a patient. The reason for this is to remind you that you are in business to sell. Unless you are in a philanthropic endeavor, your GOAL is to make money. In order to get there, you need a staff that is able to sell. That is what generates income, pays the bills, pays you and your staff and is the ruler by which to measure the growth and success of your business.

Although your staff may possess an in depth knowledge of optics and may be very knowledgeable as to what products are available and best suited to your customers, are they able to convey that knowledge to your customer in such a way that it will generate sales? Is your staff making recommendations and suggesting additional pairs of glasses? The talent that is most important to any business is the ability to sell. As I will mention throughout this course, there is a big difference between providing the customer with whatever they came in to purchase, and selling. The former is facilitating a sale whereas the latter is related to the art of selling. Imagine, if you will, when you drive through a fast food line, the person asks, "Did you want fries with your order?" or the waiter who asks, "Would you like to order some wine with dinner?" or "Can I get you some coffee or dessert?" The reason they do that is to generate income for the owner but also, they realize that the larger the check, the larger their tip. When you buy a suit or a dress, a good sales person will ask if you need a shirt and/or tie with your new suit, or a purse or belt to go with the new dress. In my opinion, when seeking new staff for your business, you are better served hiring a good salesperson and teaching them optics, than someone with optical knowledge who is unable to sell. Consider offering your staff a commission on multiple pairs or generated sales as opposed to a commission on all sales. Employees need to be reminded that their job and the reason for their pay check are to be there and to service your customer. On the other hand, that you are willing and all too happy to show your gratitude for a job above and beyond.

Most business owners assume that their staff has the ability and the talent to sell eyewear. In most cases, sales are not achieved because of the staff, but rather, in spite of the staff. Though most people are able to facilitate a sale, very few are able to generate sales. The fact that someone has been doing something a long time doesn't necessarily mean that they're good at it or doing all that could be done. Proper training will help to maximize your staff's abilities and increase your business' potential. Very often, business owners and their staff lose sight of what it is they are selling. Before we can sell our products, we need to sell ourselves. Your confidence and

product knowledge puts the customer at ease and makes the sale proceed more smoothly. If you have lost the customer's confidence, chances are you have lost the sale. You don't have multiple opportunities to sell yourself. Just as you size up your customer and determine how you are going to sell them, your customer has sized you up in the first 30-60 seconds.
Remember to make the initial connection count. First and foremost, smile. Address them by name if you know it, if you don't, don't be afraid to ask them their name and then proceed to address them accordingly.

Marketing

What do you think is the most important asset in your business?

- The most important asset is most often the one that is most overlooked, and that is your own customer base.

- This is the asset that you need to build upon and nurture. When used wisely, this alone can increase annual sales by as much as 20%.

- Anyone who has had experience with developing advertising campaigns will tell you that none of the advertising works unless you repeat it regularly and keep your name in front of the customer.

- One of the reasons that so many people use magnets as a form of advertising is because people will usually put it up on their refrigerator and forget about it... until they need it. Though they may never "look" at the magnet, they "see" it every day. I wouldn't recommend using magnets as your only form of advertising, but it is one of many that actually work. Companies also use things like note pads, personalized pens, calendars, etc.

People like to be remembered.

People like to know that you care enough about them to stay on top of their needs. Email is an excellent way to stay in touch with your customer.
It is important to capture all of their contact information, including email and their date of birth.

- Send them a birthday card or email.
- Ask them if they would like to be kept informed of new products and services as they become available.
- Send out an annual recall
- Inform your customers about specials, sales, trunk shows, etc.
- Thank them for referrals and send them an offer or a gift

Ask them about hobbies, sports, activities and any specific needs they might have
Consider informing them when specialty lenses and frames that might serve their needs, become available.

Networking

- Always carry your business cards with you
- Attend networking opportunities in your area
    - Chamber of commerce
    - Jaycees
    - Rotary

These are ideal business opportunities to network and to talk about your business and what you have to offer, as well as differences between you and others in your field.

Not to be overlooked are social opportunities. I don't recommend that you start passing business cards at your best friend's wedding, however, invariably people enter into conversations and the subject of, "What do you do?" comes up. This is an opportunity to just hand them a card and say, "If you ever need anything, please feel free to give me a call." If a conversation about eyewear should ensue, all the better, if not, you've done what you could, and any more than that could be construed as "in poor taste".
- Weddings
- Parties
- Bars
- Places of Worship

- Ask your customers to post reviews on websites like Yelp, Facebook and LinkedIn
- Create an email template for your business that includes links to your website as well as social media making it easier for your customers to access those sites on your behalf.
- Whenever you send an email, make sure to use your template and to thank your customer for the opportunity to serve their needs.

Cost of Acquiring a New Customer

- Think about what it costs your company to acquire new customers. Whether it's newspaper, direct mail, television or radio, the cost of acquiring a new customer is significant.
- It costs 6-7 times more to acquire a new customer than it does to maintain a returning customer.
    - Once you have acquired a new customer, it is important to capture that customer's information so that you can effectively market to your own patient base. A frequent buyer program is just one way to maintain customer loyalty.

- Stay in touch with your customers. Whether it's a recall once a year, an email campaign informing them of specials or new products or just a hello to let them know that you are still thinking about them and that you value their business, communication is important.
- Take advantage of things like the internet and social media to keep yourself current. Learn about your customers' needs and inform them of new products and technology that might serve those needs. Today's social media offers many opportunities to network if properly used.

Customer Service

If I asked you what you think makes a company GREAT, what would your answer be?

- What makes you decide to shop in the stores that you choose to shop?
- What has caused you to stop shopping at some of the stores that you used to frequent and no longer shop?

The answer is really quite simple. It's customer service.

- People continue to frequent a store because of it and they stop because of a lack of it.
- Niemen Marcus is a prime example of exemplary customer service.
- Most of us are familiar with the story of the customer who went back to the store and demanded a refund for tires that he had purchased there and was given a full refund, even though Niemen Marcus never sold tires. Yes, this is an extreme case and perhaps even an urban legend, but it shows the kind of service that defines Nieman Marcus.

- Most of us might also remember the Sears slogan, "Satisfaction Guaranteed or Your Money Back". There were no disclaimers, no fine print. If you were unhappy with a purchase FOR ANY REASON, AT ANY TIME, they would give you a full refund, no questions asked. Do these guarantees get abused? Absolutely. However, in the grand scheme of things, abuse was minimal, these stores had unparalleled customer loyalty, and very successful business models. As a matter of fact, Craftsman tools still have an unconditional lifetime guaranty and VERY loyal customers as a result.
- On the other hand, if you disappoint a customer just one time, you will probably lose them forever
- I once worked for someone who never spent a dime on advertising.
    - The person I worked for would replace any pair of glasses if the customer was unhappy for any reason.
    - He would warranty in full, any defective frame or lens issues, even if it wasn't covered by the company.
    - If a customer came back and said they just didn't like the glasses, he would absorb the cost of the glasses and make them a new pair, in some cases, even as much as a year later.
    - Most repairs were done at no charge. Broken temples were replaced with generic temples at no charge.
    - If you feel that the only resolution is a refund, do so with a smile. His comment was, "if you have to do it anyway, a positive attitude goes a long way to satisfying a customer and will multiply the amount of referral business that will follow. "
    - He would say that exceptional customer service is the best form of advertising.

This individual had a store without a doctor; he did not fit or dispense contact lenses, did not accept insurance, and yet achieved a multi-million dollar practice, all because of service with a smile, satisfied customers and word of mouth advertising. As a result of his exceptional service and his willingness to do all Rx changes, free of charge for a period of 90 days, he was able to get the support of local ophthalmologists and their referrals.

The Unhappy Customer

Have you ever had a customer walk into your store full of people, ranting that "these are the worst glasses I've ever bought" or "what kind of junk do you people sell here" or something comparable? If so, it is important to immediately diffuse the situation.
The best thing to do is to get them away from the rest of your customers.

- Take them in back, pull them over to the side, if you are in a mall, take them out for coffee if you have to, but get them away from the rest of your customers.
- The next thing to do is, apologize for the fact that they are unhappy. It's not important whose fault it is, the bottom line is, your customer is not happy and that is something that is not acceptable. Ask them what the problem is and do whatever it takes to resolve it.
- If after your attempt to resolve it, the customer still seems dissatisfied, ask them what you can do to make them happy. No matter how unreasonable it may seem, your goal is to make them happy.

With that in mind, there are many ways to satisfy an unhappy customer.

An important part of our job is to solve problems.

Because each case is different, there is no simple advice I can give here other than to say that whatever happens, the customer needs to walk out of the store happy and with a smile on his/her face. Sometimes it can be as easy as making them an inexpensive pair of single vision glasses at no charge or matching a competitor's price.

Here is an example:

The customer complains that their new progressive lenses aren't nearly as good as their drug store readers when they're working on the computer.

When I hear things like this, I view them as an opportunity to sell an additional pair of glasses. This is an opportunity to sell what I refer to as "task specific" eyewear. I would begin by recommending a pair of progressive eyewear with an intermediate Rx on the top going into a reading Rx, like the Essilor Computer Lens. I also have the option of recommending a lined bifocal or the Essilor Anti-Fatigue lenses. If financial issues are of concern, a single vision pair of glasses for computer use, in the customers Rx is another option.

In the event that the customer continues to complain, here is another scenario:

In your opinion, which is the better option for your business?
1. Make the customer a free pair of single vision glasses with a retail value of $100-$200
2. Give the customer a refund of $50-$100
3. Offer the customer a discount on his/her next eyewear purchase
    - My first choice would be to offer the customer a discount on the next purchase.
    - My next choice would be to make them a free pair of single vision glasses.

- I could find them a frame that costs between $10-$20 and a pair of single vision lenses only costs about $5-$10.
- This option is better than a refund. It costs me less and offering a pair of glasses that retails from $100-$200, has a much greater perceived value to the customer.

• Finally, if I need to give the customer some sort of refund, I would do so with a smile.

Remember the adage, "When handed lemons, make lemonade". By satisfying an unhappy customer, I have often gained extreme loyalty and in many cases, converted what might have been a request for a refund, into an additional sale and increased revenue.

Just imagine how you would like to be treated, and then treat your customer accordingly. After all, we all want to be treated as if we were special. Fighting with a customer makes no sense and you will never win, EVER!!!

The 2 most important rules regarding customers and customer service are:

1. The customer is never wrong
2. In the event that the customer is indeed wrong, see rule #1

Education

I find nothing more annoying than asking a store employee, questions about a product or service, and realizing that they have no clue as to either what I'm asking or as to what they're saying. Due to a lack of knowledge on their part, they appear to make the answers up as they go along or simply say, "I don't know", with no regard for my inquiry. This is a result of both poor management and training on the part of the employer, or a lack of interest and/or motivation on the part of the employee, both of which are, in my estimation, inexcusable. This could be so easily resolved with a simple, "I'm sorry, I don't know the answer, but let me get someone who does, to answer your questions."

I understand that everyone has to start somewhere and that sometimes, we may not know the answer to a particular question. An old friend once taught me that being intelligent doesn't necessarily mean knowing the answer to everything, but rather, knowing where to find it. A lack of knowledge is better served with a bit of research rather than a wrong answer.

- Certification is one way of letting our customers know that we care enough about our profession to be the best that we can be.
  - Let your customer know that Illinois does not have a licensing or certification requirement and that you chose to seek certification in order to separate yourself from those who have little or no optical knowledge, and call themselves opticians
- Look into continuing education courses, both online and at conferences in your area
  - With so many new innovations and so much new technology, it's important to be familiar with all of the latest improvements in eye care, in order that you might present your patients with the best solution for their individual needs
- Join your associations
  - Membership is just another way of letting customers know that you are active in your field and that you care about your chosen profession
  - It will get you discounts in continuing education courses and will keep you abreast of what is going on in our industry.
- Read the trade journals
  - They will show you the latest in fashions, trends, materials, designs and whatever is trending
- Consider role playing with fellow staff members

- It will make you more comfortable with changes in your presentation and delivery of new techniques.
- It's a great way to get feedback in order to create a smoother flow in your delivery. This is a way to get the entire staff be on the same page so that there are no conflicting comments within the practice.
- Use this method to present each other with examples of customer's complaints and effective ways to resolve conflict
- Talk to your reps
- They have all the latest information on their materials, designs, trends, colors, etc. All of that information is useful when selling their product.
- Use POP wherever applicable.
    - These companies have already done the research, spent the money, and make available to you, tools to assist in your sales. After all, their success is partially based on your success.
- Use any demonstration devices available to you, i.e. polarized lens demonstrator, digital lens demonstrator, etc.
- Today's consumer is much savvier than the customers of old.
    - With the advent of the internet, they are doing their own research, comparing prices on things like coatings, frames and lenses.
    - They are reading other peoples reviews on things like AR, Hi Index, Digital design progressives, free form lenses, aspheric lenses, designer frames and more.

- When asked a question by the customer, if you don't know the answer, don't make one up. Chances are, they already know the answer and they're checking on you and your knowledge. If you lie to a customer, you've lost them forever.
- If you educate them properly, without sounding superior, you have gained a customer for life.

I can't count how many times in my career I have had customers return to me and say, "I bought my glasses from you because you knew what you were talking about and it sounded like you cared?"

Celebrate the Differences

- What makes you different from your competition?
    - Do you think it's something your customer wants to or needs to know? If so, don't be afraid to tell them.
    - Are you certified or licensed?
    - How long are you in the field?
    - Do you have any awards or special recognition?
    - Does your store have a larger selection?
    - Can you produce eyewear faster than your competition?
    - Do you use newer technology or better quality materials?
    - What are your guarantees?
    - How long has your office been in business?
    - Do you know your competition?
        - If not, drop by and take a look and see what they have to offer and do so on a regular basis
        - What do your businesses have in common?
        - How do your businesses differ?

- Compare selection, service, education or familiarity with their product.
- Never demean your competition.
  - It makes you look bad and petty.
  - It opens the door to them doing the same to you.

Customers take a dim view of people speaking ill of others. There's nothing wrong with telling your customer that your competition is very good, but you are better because....

Sales

Value Your Customer

- When a customer walks into your store, what dollar value do you place on that customer? In other words, how much do you think that customer will produce in sales?
- A new customer will spend between $100 and a few thousand dollars for multiple pairs on an initial sale. If you have satisfied the customer and he comes back to the store, he will spend many hundreds or thousands in your store over his lifetime. Now multiply that by family members, friends, referrals, their families and friends and so on. So now, the customer who only might have spent $100 on the initial sale is valued in the multiple thousands of dollars over his or her lifetime. Failure to think in this way is a failure for your business.

A satisfied customer is more valuable than any advertising campaign you could conceive. It is important to remember, that statistically, a satisfied customer will tell 3 people, whereas an unhappy customer will tell 10 people.

Are You a Salesperson or An Order Taker?

A 10 year old can sell the customer what the customer wants. What makes a sales professional is leading the sale or guiding the sale and, as the professional, filling the customer needs. Sometimes, it also means making them aware of what their needs actually are.

On the other hand, over selling a customer is just as bad as under selling them.
I'm sure you've heard the term "buyer's remorse".
That's what happens when the customer walks out of the store and starts to regret what they purchased or the amount they spent. This is a fine line that a true sales professional learns to differentiate.

In any business, there are 2 options. One can either go to work or one can come to work? You might ask, "What's the difference?"

-
  - Going to work just means showing up at the workplace and going through the motions of earning one's salary.
  - Coming to work means arriving at the workplace, properly attired and well-manicured and ready to do your job in a professional manner.
    - Hair combed
    - No chipped nail polish
    - Business casual attire

Greeting Your Customer

- Remember to smile and project a positive attitude. It's contagious. You'll generate excitement about their new eyewear purchase, which can lead to a more positive shopping experience, the possibility of multiple sales and a loyal customer who'll remember you when it comes time for future purchases.
- When a customer enters your store, stop whatever it is you're doing and greet them immediately.

- Never forget, they are not an interruption of your work, they are the reason for your work.
- If they're not there, neither are you.
- If you are on the phone, politely ask if you could call the person back when you are through with the customer who walked in.
- The customer in your store is cash in hand.

Telephone

- Sometimes, your first contact with a customer is over the phone. Getting the phone customer to come into your store is as much an art as face to face sales.
- When your telephone rings, answer it before the third ring. Any longer than that and the customer begins to grow impatient.
- When talking on the phone, smile and be upbeat. It comes across over the phone.
- Always introduce yourself to the person on the other end of the phone.
- When you answer the phone, smile. A smile on your face does come across, even on the phone. Though they can't see you, you are creating an identity over the phone enabling the customer to feel that they are talking to a person, not an organization.
- Answer questions as thoroughly as possible
- If you need to call the customer back, apologize for the delay and call them back as quickly as possible
- Use their name in conversation with them. Show respect for your customer and unless directed otherwise, address them by Mr., Ms., Dr., etc. Respect is always appreciated.
- If a customer walks in, don't be afraid to ask if you could call them back. The customer in your store can see you are on the phone, but the customer on the phone

17

can't see that you have a customer. The important thing is to call the customer back as soon as possible.

Why do people buy the things they buy?

- Why do people buy luxury items instead of something functional and/or practical?

- Why do people buy name brands like Rolex or a Mercedes Benz or designer products?

- What motivates people to buy?

The basic answer to all of the above questions is outlined in Maslow's Hierarchy of Needs.

- People buy the things they need for survival and existence. In the case of eyewear, they need it to see properly. It is a health item, a prescription.
- People buy things that give them a sense of safety or security. Today, more and more people are buying eyewear to protect their eyes from the harmful effects of UV. This is one of the reasons that educating our customers is so important.
- The next thing that motivates people to buy is how they look in their eyewear and if it improves their physical image. Customers are also motivated by their desire to appear more attractive and to be accepted by the people they care about and people with whom they come into contact.
- One of the reasons that they select the eyewear that they select reflects directly on their sense of having reached a certain economic status and increasing their self-esteem. This is also about using status symbols to gain recognition and respect for their achievement's, whether those achievements are real or perceived. People buy things to make themselves feel better.

- Finally, eyewear is just one more way for people to express their individuality and their creativity. This is their way of expressing their identity and uniqueness.

Lens Extras

Today's many lens options should be viewed as opportunities to better serve our customers because of our ability to satisfy all their eye care needs and, as a result, generate sales:

Coating Options	Lens Types	Special Use	Occupational lenses	Frames
Specialty Tints	Safety lenses	Dive masks	Anti-Fatigue lenses	Plastic frames with adjustable pads
Polarized Transitions	Poly Carbonate	Shooting glasses	Computer Lenses	Titanium frames
Premium AR	Hi Index	Motorcycle glasses Day and Night	Double Seg	Rimless
Blue Blocker	Trifocals	Sports glasses	Reading Glasses	Colors
UV	Progressives	Ski goggles		Flexon
				Interchangeable Lenses

The following **top five tips from the NYSOA** may help prevent eye and vision damage from overexposure to UV radiation:

- Wear protective eyewear any time the eyes are exposed to UV rays, even on cloudy days and during the winter.
- Look for quality sunglasses or contact lenses that offer good protection. Sunglasses or protective contact lenses should block 99 to 100 percent of UV-A and UV-B radiation and screen out 75 to 90 percent of visible light.
- Check to make sure sunglass lenses are perfectly matched in color and free of distortions or imperfections.
- Purchase gray-colored lenses as they reduce light intensity without altering the color of objects and therefore provide the most natural color vision. Brown or amber-colored lenses may be better for those who are visually impaired since they increase contrast as well as reducing light intensity.
- Don't forget protection for young children and teenagers. They typically spend more time in the sun than adults and are at a greater risk for damage.

Children need protection too

- Most businesses consider children's eyewear as an insignificant necessity rather than a practice building tool.
- They fail to realize that if they capture the child's business, they will likely capture the parent as well.
- Parents appreciate having their children treated with respect and valuing their business.
- One of the best ways to capture their business is to have a large selection of frames from which children can select.
- If you can, try to create a kid friendly area

- Offer them package pricing which includes a comprehensive warranty.
- Children are a great opportunity to offer a spare pair, sunglasses and sports glasses. Sports glasses with transition lenses can serve both purposes.
- Remember to address the most important law of Maslow's Hierarchy when presenting children's eyewear. Need and Health
- "The lenses of children's eyes are more transparent than those of adults allowing shorter wavelength light to reach the retina," said Dr. Lagana. "Because the effects of solar radiation are cumulative, it's important to develop good protection habits early, such as purchasing proper sunglasses for young children and teenagers."
- According to the NYSOA, parents should purchase sunglasses for all children including infants.
- The American Eye-Q® survey found 66 percent of Americans purchase sunglasses for their children, but more than one in four parents do not check to make sure the lenses have proper UV protection.
- Additionally, less than one-third (29 percent) of parents make sure their child wears sunglasses while outdoors.

This is a market that is virtually untapped by most eye care professionals. In addition to generating additional income, this market will also build customer loyalty. Parents appreciate knowing that you care enough about their children, to address these issues.

With today's aging population, things like macular degeneration, glaucoma, cataracts, retinal damage, etc. are becoming much more prevalent and creating more opportunities to generate sales when properly presented.

- One example of this is Anti-Reflective Coatings. An interesting statistic is that in Europe, 65% of eyewear

purchases include AR coatings. In Japan, the number jumps to 90%. In the United States, that number is a paltry 15%, although todays chain stores have increased this number to as much as 50%.
- I attribute this disparity to a lack of knowledge on the part of the dispenser in the presentation of AR. Instead of merely asking, "Do you want Anti-reflective coating on your new eyewear?" Most customers will either ask "How much is it?" and then say, "No, I don't need it" or "What does it do?" and in most cases, receive inaccurate or inadequate information and then reject it.
- When I present AR coatings, I have the customer look at my glasses and then show them an uncoated pair. I let them know that uncoated lenses only allow between 85% TO 92% light transmission and that AR coating allows more light through the lens, allowing for clearer, sharper vision, particularly for night driving.
- I have sometimes heard objections, like they're so hard to keep clean, at which time I inform them of the new hydrophobic coatings available. As a result, I sell 95% of my customers, the premium AR lenses. Remember, always offer the best.

Making the Sale

- An important part of making the sale is proper marketing within your own store.
    - Keep your store clean and dust free.
    - Keep your floors clean
    - Check your windows and displays, making sure to keep them clean and organized
    - Keep your better frames towards the front of your store and your budget frames towards the back
    - Keep your better frames at eye level
    - Use visual aids

- If a picture is worth a thousand words, a physical sample is the equivalent of a novel
- Keep a sample of high index lenses mounted in a frame, comparing comparable prescriptions in different materials
- Keep a sample of the different anti-reflective lenses available, mounted in a frame with one coated lens and one uncoated
- Keep a sample of photochromatic lenses with a light to demonstrate the photochromatic properties
  - Make sure you tell the customer the benefits as well as the drawbacks. Your customer will not be happy when they find out that the lenses won't change in the car
  - Let them know that the lenses are also affected by temperature and therefore they will be darker in winter than in summer
- Group frames by price
  - One of the things I've seen in optical stores is frames that are displayed without regard to price, e.g. expensive frames and budget frames displayed together. This detracts greatly from the better quality frames.

- Group frames by vendor
  - When creating displays, less is more. A small grouping by a particular designer

makes a greater impact and highlights that designer, letting the customer know that this product is special.

Engage Your Customer in Conversation

- Ask the customer if they have their prescription.
- If they do, ask to see it. It will assist you in selecting the proper frame to suit the RX. It also tells you whether they are ready to purchase glasses.
- If they don't have an RX and there is a doctor on the premises, recommend an exam.
- Remind your customer that an exam is not merely for a prescription, it is also to check the health of the eyes and is a method to detect other diseases, like glaucoma, diabetes, macular degeneration, diabetes, high blood pressure, MS, heart disease and more.
- Find out what your customer does for a living. This will enable you to suggest the products best suited to your customer
- This applies particularly to your customer's sports and hobby and general lifestyle issues.
- When it's time to make a sale, start by greeting your customer with a smile. A smile on your face is more likely to lighten things up than trying to come across as too serious.
    - Although it's important to be professional, never talk down to the customer, but on the other hand, don't use terminology that the customer doesn't understand. I have often heard a customer ask their optician, "What are you measuring" to hear the optician answer "I'm measuring your PD" Do you really think they know what a PD is? Tell them instead, "I'm measuring the distance between your eyes, so that we can place the center of the lenses directly in front of each eye in order to get the

clearest, sharpest vision, with the least distortion".
- When you make your initial contact with your customer, ask them their name and tell them your name.
- Offer them a business card with your name on it. If they're shopping, they are more likely to ask for you when they come back
- During your sales presentation, let the customer know a little about your qualifications, i.e. how long you've been in the field or any information you can offer them to let them know that you are more than just a glorified sales person.

Observe Your Customer

- Do you know what kind of car they drive? Do they wear jewelry? Are they wearing a quality watch or a practical one? Is your customer carrying a designer purse? How much attention does your customer pay to her make-up? This will at least give you an inkling of this customers attitude toward luxury or practicality
- How do they hold their heads? This will help you when measuring for a multifocal lens.
- What are some of the other things that you look for when observing your customer?
- As important as this is, I can't stress enough that this is only a guideline or starting point. No matter what you observe, don't assume anything. Though they may be driving a Mercedes or wearing a Rolex, they may have lost their jobs and are no longer able to afford luxury items. That is not to say that they shouldn't be presented the best, just don't assume anything.
- The most important things are to listen and to observe the customer.

- At this stage, listen, observe, and don't talk. There is a reason we were given 2 eyes, 2 ears and 1 mouth. Pay attention to the customer. Long ago, my father taught me something I'll never forget, "The more you talk, the more likely you are to say something you shouldn't".
- Listen to what they are telling you. Hear what they are telling you. Address what they are telling you. Listening serves no purpose if you ignore what they say. They are giving you all the information you need. Use it.
- Look for an opportunity to sell additional pairs or upgraded lenses and/or coatings.

Something very important to remember throughout everything you do is "Never ask a question that you don't want to hear the answer to".

- Something that makes me crazy is hearing a salesperson ask, "Would you like to leave a deposit?" What they should say is, "How would you like to pay for that?"
- Another one is, "Did you want a plastic or metal frame?" Why would you want to eliminate half your inventory before you've even started? If they want something specific, they will tell you.
- Think about this. "Are you interested in a spare pair?" versus "Is your spare pair current?" Leading the conversation in the direction you want to take it is what separates a successful salesperson from an order taker.
- Always, always, show your best first. The reasons for that are very simple.
    - Everything they try on after that will be compared to the first one.
        - It's easier to come down in price than it is to go up.
- Never assume how much a customer is willing to spend. Prejudging what you think a customer is willing

to spend is one of the worst mistakes a salesperson can make.
- People tend to buy wants more than needs. After all, does a woman need 10 purses, 30 pairs of shoes, or does a man need 10 suits, 20 pairs of pants, a new cell phone every year or 2, etc. Look at how many people buy convertibles. That's not something that's going to get us to our destination any faster or safer.
- Let the customer know that a quality frame will last a lot longer than an inexpensive frame and that it can be reused in the future for future RX changes, as a result, an expensive frame, amortized over its life is less expensive than an inexpensive frame and therefore, a much better value.
- Explain the features and benefits of the products you are recommending.
    - People don't mind paying for things if they understand how it benefits them, they do however, object to paying for something that has no perceived value to them.
    - Make them see the value. I have often used the example of my experiences in Europe and seeing that people, who earn less money than Americans, buy better cars, more expensive clothing, better quality eyewear, etc. When I asked them why in the world they would do that, the answer I always heard was, "Unlike Americans, we can't afford to buy over and over, so we buy once, we buy the best, and it lasts forever." There is a reason that people buy Mercedes, BMW, Cartier, Tiffany, etc.
    - I tell people that a quality designer will not allow his name to be associated with a poor quality product, and therein lies the reason for the higher price, as well as the need to pay the

designer his share, but to remember, that a designer's name usually denotes quality.
- Selling quality will result in increased revenue and profits.
- Keep in mind that you are not selling price, you are selling quality
- Progressive lenses offer vision at all distances, no lines, latest technology, smooth transition from far to near, etc.
- Anti-reflective coatings offer better night vision, reduced glare from headlights at night and on rainy days and nights, increased light transmission, reduced glare from computer screens, in photos, etc.
- Polarized lenses eliminate reflective glare on the road and on water

If you are asked a question, for which you are not prepared, under no circumstances should you ever just make something up. Recently, I was in a restaurant and heard a customer ask her waiter what the difference was between a vodka martini and a vodka tonic. His answer was "they use a different mix". Someone, overhearing the conversation, corrected the waiter. That waiter lost all credibility.

- Gaining a customer's confidence is a difficult task. Regaining lost confidence is next to impossible. A customer would rather hear, "I'm not quite sure, let me find out for you and get back to you". Of course, I can't stress enough, the importance of follow up.
- If you want to sell high end eyewear, it's important that you lead by example and wear high end eyewear. Whether you need prescription eyewear or not, if you are selling them, you should be wearing them. Ask your reps, they will be happy to sell you a frame at a

discount, to get you to wear their frames. Sometimes, they might even give you one for free.
- For a long time now, eyewear has become a fashion accessory and Planos have been referred to as attitude glasses. Eyewear can age a young person, make him/her appear more professional or can simply enhance their appearance just like a piece of jewelry. Eyewear is jewelry for the face.
- Keep fashion magazines and pictures of celebrities wearing the latest eyewear, available in the waiting or sales area.
- Avoid saying things like, "These glasses will go with everything." That makes selling another pair more difficult. Also, avoid saying "Those glasses go very well with your hair/eyes." Usually those things don't change. Instead, say things like, "Your new eyewear looks great with a business suit." or "Your new eyewear goes very well with what you're currently wearing".
- Generate excitement by saying things like, "We just got some new things in this week, let me show you."
- Know the buzz words. Use them where they're applicable, but more importantly, be familiar with the terms the customers might be familiar with.

Say	**Instead of**
Eyewear	Glasses
Previous or returning customer	Old customer
Sales associate	Girl
Optician	Technician
One moment please	Just a minute
Tailored	Plain
Youthful	Cute
Stylish	Nice
Inexpensive	Cheap
Excellent Value	Expensive
Geek Chic	Nerdy
Fashion forward	Avant garde or modern

- Retro
- Vintage
- Impact resistant
- Scratch resistant
- Retired

Old fashioned
Old style
Unbreakable
Scratch proof
Discontinued

The Internet Shopper

Today, most everyone starts their shopping excursions on the internet. The customer researches the products, the styles, the reviews and the prices.
This is a situation that arises in every practice. How would you handle a customer that says, "I saw the same thing on the internet for $30 less than your price?
This is a difficult situation because the customer assumes we are gouging them. They might ask you if you will meet competitor's prices. If you market your business properly, you will probably have told your customer that you will meet or beat any competitor's prices.
My solution to this problem is:
1. I explain to the customer that as a brick and mortar store, my expenses are obviously higher than the internet
2. The internet often charges shipping
3. In the event there is a problem in the future, I can offer things like warranties, adjustments, repairs, etc.
4. The internet can be a hazard due to the amount of counterfeits in the industry
5. If I have the product in stock, they can take it with them rather than waiting
6. I will offer to reduce the price, usually splitting the difference or if I need to, going so far as to meet the price.

I want to remind you again, what is the value of that customer over a lifetime and what does it cost me to acquire a new customer?

This is my secret weapon!!!

As simple as this may seem, it works!!! One way that I have found to be almost foolproof in selling additional eyewear to customers, whether they are coming in for a repair, a dispense, or an adjustment, is to say to them, "I realize that you may not be in the market for eyewear today, but when you are, please let me know, because I have something that I think would look great on you." Invariably, the customer will say, "show it to me". Now if you are good at what you do, and are good at picking frames for your customers, you stand a 1 in 5 chance of selling an additional pair.
- After you have selected the first pair and while you are writing up the sale, ask the customer if they have a spare pair. If you can't sell them a spare, perhaps they want to update their old ones.
    - "How are your sunglasses?"
    - "What kind of eyewear do you wear for golf?"
    - "Do you have your prescription in your scuba mask/ski goggles/sports glasses?"

If you ask these questions, you will sell 1 in 4. Even if they are not buying multiple pairs today, it's important to plant the seed for future sales opportunities. If you don't ask, you are an order taker and are costing your employer a lot of money. On the other hand, if you increase your sales by 25%, which is a minimum, you can ask your employer for a raise and prove your value.

You've shown your best, you've talked about the benefits and the features of the product, the customer likes the product, make sure you have addressed any issues that they might have, now is the time to stop talking and close the sale. "I think your selection is excellent and I know you'll be happy with your new eyewear. All I ask is that you tell your friends where you got them and the next time I see you, let me know how many compliments you got."

Turn Overs

Something else that is very important in any sales position, is realizing that sometimes there may be personality conflicts. After all, no one gets along with everyone. Occasionally, people just don't click together. There are also situations where we feel like we've shown the customer everything we have to offer, or have answered all of their questions, yet we sense that the customer is not happy with us, for whatever the reason may be. This is a situation that is best handled with something called a "Turn over".
"I'm sorry Mrs. Grey. Let me see if perhaps one of my associates has any suggestions." Calling over one of your associates, perform the proper introductions and say, "Mrs. Grey, this is Jane, we've worked together for a long time and perhaps she can make a suggestion." "Jane, this is Mrs. Grey and she is looking for a frame for evening wear. Do you have any suggestions?" Then walk away.

Task Specific Eyewear

Task specific eyewear is often overlooked.
If a customer doesn't get it, I ask them,
- o "How many pairs of shoes do you own? How many black pairs?
- o You have one pair for dress, one pair for casual, one pair for sports, etc. You have brown shoes for your brown clothes, black shoes for your black clothes, etc.? And yet, you have one pair of glasses to go along with everything?
- o What do people see first, your feet or your face?
- o Today's eyewear is a fashion accessory, like jewelry for the face."
- Keep these things in mind,
  - o If you don't ask, you don't get

- If you don't ask the question, the answer is always, NO.
- Would you wear your gym shoes with your suit or your dress shoes to play tennis? Would you wear your golf shoes to the pool?
- Ultra violet light is one of the causes of macular degeneration and the early onset of cataracts. Sunglasses are necessary to protect our eyes from the harmful effects of UV.
- Based on the customer's individual needs, he/she might want a pair for everyday that might be more fun and something different for a work environment.
- An important issue today is computer fatigue which is something that affects many eyeglass wearers, regardless of age, who spend a lot of time on the computer. Macular Degeneration is another increasing problem among the elderly and there are tints that can assist customers with vision issues.

Occupational Eyewear

Often overlooked, is eyewear to suit the customers occupational needs.

Style	Profession
Double D Seg	Electrician
	Carpenter
	Commercial Pilots
Computer eyewear	Computer users
D35-D40 Bi or Tri	Architect
Polarized lenses	Fisherman
	Boaters
	Drivers/ Chauffers
Golf bifocal	Golfers
Safety eyewear	Woodworkers/Hobbyists/Factory

Make the Customer Your Own
- After you have made the sale, make the customer your own by sending them a thank you card. Tell them how much you appreciate the fact that they chose you over your competition.
- Something that is often overlooked is the final dispense. The final impression is just as important as the initial impression. It is important to let the customer know that you care enough to put on the finishing touches and that service continues even after the purchase.

Very often, I see eyewear being dispensed without a proper adjustment. Take a couple of minutes to check the adjustment. It is alright to ask the customer how the glasses feel, but even if everything seems acceptable to the customer, if you see something that needs to be addressed, do so now. After all, the customer is not the expert, you are. Giving the customer the glasses without a final adjustment, is the same as being sold a pair of pants that aren't hemmed and being expected to walk out of the store wearing them that way. The work is not complete. Telling a customer that you just want to make a slight adjustment shows the customer that you care about their experience.

- Instructing all customers on the proper care of their eyewear is another technique that is often overlooked. This is particularly true as it relates to children's eyewear and is greatly appreciated by the parents.
- When you have finished, remind the customer that you do not charge for minor repairs and adjustments and encourage them to come back to you when they need service, or just to stop in every 6 months for a tune up. When they come in, tighten their screws, adjust their frames, change their nose pads, clean their glasses, etc. Basically, show them that your service is superior to others. Remember, every time they come into your store is another opportunity to make a sale.
- When dispensing a multifocal lens to a new multifocal wearer, I can't stress enough, the importance of proper

instruction of what to expect and proper usage. This makes an enormous impact on the success or failure of a first time multifocal wearer.
- Offer them a discount on a future purchase. Tell them how much you would appreciate a referral or a comment on yelp or other social media.
- Offer them a gift card if they refer a friend. A $10 gift card at a Starbucks, for example, for them and their friend is a very inexpensive cost of acquiring a new customer and is always appreciated.

Nobody Walks

Last, but certainly not least is the rule NOBODY WALKS!!!!

- If a customer walks in to buy eyewear, you need to be aware that if they don't buy from you, they are going to buy from someone.
- If the customer has an issue with the price, offer them a discount if you need to. Again, I want to remind you to value that customer. Now think about how much money just walked out your door.
- It is better to discount the eyewear and view the discount as the cost of acquisition, rather than let it walk out your door.
- Your employer's daily expenses remain relatively fixed
  - If a pair of eyewear retails for $500 it might cost between $150-$200. Although not something I recommend on a regular basis, isn't it better to sell it for $300 than to let the customer walk?

You've made a $100 and gained a customer. Again I remind you, what is that customer and any referrals he might send you, worth to your business over a lifetime?

— The last words you should tell a customer who is walking out of your store should be, "If you find something you like elsewhere, we would be happy to order it for you and we guarantee to beat anyone else's price".

Few will come back, but at least you've left the door open and given yourself half a chance. That is why it is so important to make the sale on initial contact.

Do what you love

- Do what you love, and love what you do. It makes going to work a lot more fun and less of a chore. If you don't enjoy your work, your customer will sense it and you will have lost their confidence. Once lost, it is nearly always impossible to retrieve.

- If you don't like what you do, get out. You can't possibly be good doing something you don't like and you won't be happy going to work, day after day.

- On the other hand, if you like what you do, you will make it fun, entertaining and engaging, and it won't feel like you're going to work. You will draw the customer in with your enthusiasm and make them as enthusiastic as you are.

www.ingramcontent.com/pod-product-compliance
Lightning Source LLC
Chambersburg PA
CBHW070725020526
44116CB00031B/1917